GW00993146

THE

Little Book

OF

FAIRIES

In the same series

THE

Little Book

— OF —

FAIRIES

ANNA FRANKLIN
& PAUL MASON

© Vega 2003

Text © Anna Franklin 2003

Condensed extracts from The Illustrated Encyclopaedia
of Fairies by Anna Franklin, illustrated by Paul Mason
and Helen Field.

ISBN 1-84333-688-X

A catalogue record for this book is available
from the British Library

Published in 2003 by
Vega
64 Brewery Road
London, N7 9NT
Visit our website at www.chrysalisbooks.co.uk

A member of Chrysalis Books plc

Editor: Alison Moss
Designer: Andrew Sutterby
Production: Susan Sutterby

Printed & bound in China by
Hong Kong Graphics & Printing Ltd

Contents

Introduction

The figure of the fairy continues to intrigue and enchant us, although today most people would consider fairies as merely a suitable bedtime tale for children. But only a few hundred years ago belief in fairies was absolute in every stratum of society. Every tree, rock, hill, meadow, stream or lake contained a spirit in the form of a nymph which had to be placated if the meadow was to be ploughed, the tree cut down, the hill built upon, or the water taken from the stream or lake. Fairy goodwill had to be kept by the correct methods of address, the right offerings and the keeping of taboos. Stories of the fairies are rooted in an age that shared a world-view very different from the materialistic one we entertain today. It is generally accepted that the English word 'fairy' or 'faerie' is derived, by way of the French 'fée', from the Latin 'fatare' meaning 'to enchant'. Variations on the spelling of fairy include fayerye, fairye, fayre and faery. The word 'faërie' was originally the term for enchantment and only latterly came to refer to the race. It was more common to refer to a fay or fays. Fairies inhabit a realm that impinges on the human one but which is rarely glimpsed. Fairies themselves are seldom seen, except under special circumstances, at certain times, or by the use of particular herbs, potions or magic objects. In the past it was considered unlucky to name the fairies, or even to use the word fairy, perhaps because to do so may have summoned them, or because using a name without its owner's permission was a threat or challenge. It was wise to call them the Good People, the Little People, The Gentry, the Mother's Blessing, Good Neighbours, Wee Folk or the Hidden People.

What do fairies look like ?

Fairies come in all shapes and sizes. Some are as tiny as insects, others as large as giants. Some are very beautiful, others incredibly ugly. Some look human, others like monsters or animals. Some are invisible, and most can change shape at will, turning  into cats, dogs, horses and beautiful maidens, or even whirlwinds and wisps of fire. Many fairies don't wear clothes, and instead are often covered in hair, particularly red hair. Some are very smartly dressed in velvet and lace, while others go about in rags and are offended by gifts of clothes from well-meaning humans. Fairies usually dress in white, red and green or in earthy colours to blend in with the landscape they inhabit. Those associated with the fog dress in grey. Very few fairies have wings!

An old spell
To see fairies:

Take a pint of Sallet oil and put it in a glasse, first
washing it with rose water. Then put thereto the
budds of hollyhocke, of marygolde, of young hazle
and the topps of wild thyme.
Take the grasse of a fairy throne; then all these put
into the glasse...dissolve three dayes in the sunne,
and keep it for thy use.

Asrai are small and delicate English water fairies of Cheshire and Shropshire that melt into a pool of water when captured or exposed to sunlight. When you see the tendrils of mist that come off a body of water as the sun starts to rise, these are the asrai. They melt as the sun climbs. They also come out on the nights of the full moon to gaze at its luminous face. Such nights are called Asrai Nights. Each asrai only comes to the surface once a century. They are always female, lovely, with long green hair and webbed feet.

A fisherman once caught an asrai with the idea of selling it to the rich people at the nearby castle. Though the fairy begged for her freedom, the man hardened his heart. She touched his arm and it felt like ice, but still he rowed on, covering her with rushes. The sun had risen by the time he reached the shore and when he lifted the rushes his net was empty and all that remained was a damp patch. But the arm she had touched was paralysed the rest of his life, and nothing could warm it.

The eerie banshee appears as an omen of death or misfortune to certain Irish and Scottish families of pure Milesian descent. Her terrifying wail is a combination of a wild goose's screech, a wolf's howl, and the pitiful cry of an abandoned child. Her name simply means 'woman fairy' and she is usually seen at night in the guise of a veiled and shrouded woman, sitting in a tree combing her long hair. Beware: if one of her hairs should fall on you it is very bad luck indeed.

*C*ormoran built St Michael's Mount, an island just off the coast of Cornwall, as a dwelling for himself and his wife. He is the giant mentioned in the famous story of Jack and the Beanstalk. When Jack planted his magic beans, their shoots grew into the clouds and he was able to climb up into the giant's treasure house. Although the giant was unable to see Jack, he could smell him and cried out:

Fee fi fo fum!
I smell the blood of an Englishman –
Be he live or be he dead
I'll grind his bones to make my bread!

Jack was too clever for the giant, and by a trick killed him and stole his treasure.

When a person drowns or is buried at sea, mariners say that he or she has gone to Davy Jones's Locker.
Davy is a latter day incarnation of the spirit of the sea who may be kindly or treacherous as he chooses – just like the sea itself. Some say that sailors originally wore golden earrings so as to have an offering handy to placate the fickle sea deities, should the need arise.

Djinn are Arabian fairies mentioned in the Koran. A tradition from the Prophet says that the djinn were formed of 'smokeless fire', i.e., the fire of the wind Simoom, while others say they are the offspring of fire, with fire in their veins instead of blood. They were created 2000 years before Adam was made from earth, but will be annihilated at the Final Judgement.

There are five varieties of djinn from the very powerful Marid, to the Afreet, the Sheytans and the Jinn, to the least powerful order, the Jann.

When the Arabs poured water on the ground, let down a bucket into a well, or entered a bath, they would ask the permission of the djinn, either 'Permission?' ['Destoor'] or 'Permission, ye blessed!'

Good djinn are very beautiful but the bad ones are very ugly, although they are shapeshifters and can appear as humans, monsters, cats, ostriches, dogs and snakes. The evil djinn cause sandstorms and waterspouts.

Dryads are tree nymphs of ancient Greek myth. Their name derives from the word 'drus' meaning 'tree'. They make their homes in oak trees, leaving them on moonlit nights to dance with Artemis, the goddess of the moon, or sometimes with Dionysus, the god of wine. Their trees grow only in secluded spots where they are unlikely to be encountered. When the tree dies, so does the nymph, and if the tree is cut down a cry of anguish can be heard escaping it.

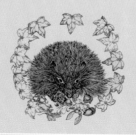

The Fachan is a Highland fairy of Glen Etive, Argyll, in Scotland. He has one eye, one hand and one leg, one ear, one arm and one toe – in fact he only has one of everything, all lined up down the centre of his body. He carries a spiked club with which he attacks any human who dares to approach his mountain realm. He hates all living creatures but especially birds, which he envies for their gift of flight.

Goblin, a word that simply means 'Spirit', is sometimes used as a generic term for the uglier and more unpleasant fairies such as boggarts, bogies, ghouls and bogles, or just mischievous house fairies. However, it may also refer to the groups of fairies that live underground, especially in churchyards, or in the clefts of rocks or among the roots of ancient trees. Then again, some claim that the race of goblins originally emerged from a cleft in the Spanish Pyrenees and proceeded to spread across Europe. They are mostly seen on Halloween, when they consort with ghosts and tempt humans to eat fairy food. Goblins sometimes appear as little deformed humans or animals. A smile from a goblin can turn milk sour or curdle the blood.

Grigs are tiny British fairies about the size of a grasshopper. They dress in green and wear red caps, which some say are made of flowers. They are always happy and jolly, hence the expression 'as merry as a grig'. In 1936, two workers were crossing Stanmore Common in Middlesex when they saw three grigs playing in the bracken. Two of them pulled on their red caps and disappeared, but the third was in such a panic that he pulled his cap too hard and fell into it as if it was a sack. One of the men reached out to pick it up, exclaiming that it was a fine red hat. The other warned him to leave it alone, but he pulled it on his head. The grig in the hat began to pull his hair and beat him about the head and the man dragged off the cap exclaiming that there was the mother and father of all hornets inside it. The grig shot out of it as it lay on the ground and cried, 'You was told to leave it lay.' All the bracken rang with the laughter of the grigs and the men fled from the common.

Jack Frost is a creature from English folklore, the personification of the spirit of winter weather who scatters ice in his wake, making the trees and grass sparkle like diamonds. He also paints windowpanes with elaborate frozen patterns and nips people's noses, fingers and toes with the grip of his chilly fingers. He always dresses entirely in white, with icicles dripping from his clothes.

Jack has counterparts wherever there is snowy weather in winter. In Russia, there is Morozko and Father Frost, the soul of winter, whose icy embrace brings death to helpless travellers. He leaps from tree to tree, snapping his fingers, causing them to be covered with frost.

Knockers are fairies that live in the tin mines of
Devon and Cornwall in south-west England.
When the mines were in operation, they sometimes
guided miners to good seams by tapping or
'knocking'. Their favours had to be rewarded with
food, traditionally a bit of pasty or tallow. However,
they were not always well disposed towards the
miners and sometimes pulled faces at them or
performed grotesque dances. Whistling offended
them, as did swearing, and brought ill luck or a
harmless shower of stones.

Knockers have been described as small, ugly and thin
limbed, with hook noses and mouths like slits, which
stretch from ear to ear. Some said that knockers
were the spirits of those who had crucified Christ
and were punished by working out their penance
below the earth. Despite this they sing carols on
Christmas Day, Easter and All Saints' Day.

The Lady of the Lake is a beautiful fairy that appears in one of the Arthurian tales. She snatched the baby Lancelot from his real mother and disappeared with him into the depths of a lake where she brought him up in her underwater kingdom, training him to become the greatest knight the world had ever seen. She also supplied King Arthur with his magical sword Excalibur, a gift from the land of the fairy, whose sheath safeguarded its owner from harm.

Some call her Vivienne; in 'Morte d'Arthur' Thomas Malory calls her Nimue, and she has also been called Niniane. She may have been one of the Gwragedd Annwn, the Welsh fairy maidens who dwell beneath lakes in underworld kingdoms.

A leprechaun is an Irish lone fairy cobbler who makes all the shoes for the fairy gentry. He possesses hidden pots of gold. Leprechaun is the Leinster name for them, although they are called Cluricane in County Cork, Luricane or Lurican in Kerry, Lurikeen in Kildare, Lurigadaune in Tipperary and Loghery-man in Ulster.

Leprechauns are small, withered, and dressed in a homely fashion. They love whiskey and tobacco – smoking small pipes. They live under the roots of trees and in deserted castles.

To get the leprechaun's legendary pot of gold away from him, you must see him before he sees you. One leprechaun showed a farmer the single ragwort in a field under which there was gold. The man marked it with a red ribbon while he went to get a shovel. When he came back there was a red ribbon on every ragwort.

Peris are the good fairies of Persia. Once a merchant's son saw four peris as they bathed at sunset in a pool. The man quickly gathered up their garments and hid them in a hollow tree. The peris searched in vain for their clothes and begged the young man to return them. He consented on condition that one should become his wife. This was agreed and he took his new wife home, carefully concealing her fairy clothing from her without which she could not escape. After 10 years he again had to travel and left the fairy in the charge of an old woman, to whom he revealed his secret. While he was away the peri cajoled the old woman into letting her put on the fairy clothes for an instant, so that she might momentarily regain her native beauty. No sooner had she put them on than she vanished.

Robin Goodfellow is a mischievous English fairy who loves to play tricks on mortals, perhaps rushing between their feet in the form of a hare, transforming himself into a horse and carrying them away, or appearing as a walking fire. He sometimes leads people astray, and in the past when someone got lost, people used to say: 'Robin Goodfellow has been with you tonight.' People so bewitched would only find their way when they turned their caps or cloaks inside out to break the spell.

He is a solitary being, with the head of a handsome youth and the body of a goat. He has a lusty nature, small horns on his head, and carries musical pipes. He is never seen between Halloween (31 October) and the vernal equinox (21 March), and is usually accompanied by a variety of animals.

A knight called Launfal fell in love with a fairy maid. Her name was Tryamour, meaning 'test of love'. She agreed to appear whenever he wished, on condition that he must never speak of her or summon her when others were present. Guinevere noticed the young man and tried to seduce him. He recoiled saying his lady put the queen's beauty to shame. Guinevere, deeply offended, complained to Arthur that Launfal had tried to rape her and the knight was immediately arrested. It was decreed that he must produce his mistress within one year or die. Of course, the fairy would no longer come, and one year later he stood in the courtyard at Camelot waiting to be executed. Then through the gate, riding on a white horse, the fairy Tryamour appeared. All agreed that he had spoken truthfully; she was indeed the loveliest woman in existence. The two lovers rode away together to Fairyland, never to be seen again.

Hollow Hills

Many fairies live beneath the ancient burial mounds, the Hollow Hills of legend, where they feast and dance. Sometimes at night, these hills are said to sparkle with light and if you press an ear to the hill, you will hear their revels.

Some of the ancient poets and bards, such as the famed Carolan, learned their craft by sleeping on fairy hills and mounds, allowing the magical music to enter their hearts and souls as they slept. Many old Irish tunes such as 'The Pretty Girl Milking the Cow' and 'The Londonderry Air' are fairy songs. It is unwise to sing or whistle such tunes near a fairy mound as the fairies don't like to hear their music on mortal lips.

Departure of the Fairies

It is said that as humans spread over the landscape, and as farms, villages and towns appeared, the fairies retreated further and further into the wilder places, perhaps eventually disappearing altogether, going into the west with the setting sun. The last Fairy Ride was witnessed at the beginning of the nineteenth century by a herdboy and his sister at a hamlet near Glen Eathie. A procession of dwarfish strangers rode by and the boy asked them who they were and where they were going. The leader replied, 'Not of the race of Adam. The people of peace shall never more be seen in Scotland.'

Picture Credits

ELF: Paul Mason.

ASPARAS: Paul Mason.

BORUTA: Paul Mason.

WHAT DO FAIRIES LOOK LIKE? & AN OLD SPELL: Figure photograph Anna Franklin, artwork Paul Mason.

ASRAI: Paul Mason.

BANSHEE: Paul Mason.

CORMORAN: Paul Mason.

DAVY JONES: Paul Mason.

DJINN: Paul Mason.

DRYADS: Paul Mason.

FACHAN: Paul Mason.

GOBLIN: Paul Mason.

GRIG: Figure photograph Anna Franklin, artwork Paul Mason.

JACK FROST: Paul Mason.

KNOCKERS: Paul Mason.

LADY OF THE LAKE: Paul Mason.

LEPRECHAUN: Paul Mason.

PERI: Figure photograph Anna Franklin.

ROBIN GOODFELLOW: Paul Mason.

TRYAMOUR: Knight photograph Anna Franklin, other photographs and artwork Paul Mason.

HOLLOW HILLS: Paul Mason.

DEPARTURE OF THE FAIRIES: Paul Mason.